a passion for
precuts

LEISURE ARTS, INC.
Little Rock, Arkansas

table of contents

Library of Congress Control Number: 2012930436

ISBN-13: 978-1-46470-188-7

EDITORIAL STAFF

Vice President of Editorial: Susan White Sullivan
Special Projects Director: Susan Frantz Wiles
Senior Prepress Director: Mark Hawkins
Art Publications Director: Rhonda Shelby
Technical Writer: Lisa Lancaster
Technical Editors: Frances Huddleston, Mary Sullivan Hutcheson, and Jean Lewis
Editorial Writer: Susan McManus Johnson
Art Category Manager: Lora Puls

Graphic Artists: Dayle Carroza, Jacob Casleton, Kara Darling, Becca Snider, Amy Temple, and Dana Vaughn
Imaging Technician: Stephanie Johnson
Prepress Technician: Janie Marie Wright
Photography Manager: Katherine Laughlin
Contributing Photographer: Ken West
Contributing Photo Stylist: Sondra Daniel
Mac Information Technology Specialist: Robert Young

BUSINESS STAFF

President and Chief Executive Officer: Rick Barton
Vice President of Sales: Mike Behar
Director of Finance and Administration: Laticia Mull Dittrich
Director of Corporate Planning: Anne Martin
National Sales Director: Martha Adams

Creative Services: Chaska Lucas
Information Technology Director: Hermine Linz
Controller: Francis Caple
Vice President, Operations: Jim Dittrich
Retail Customer Service Manager: Stan Raynor
Print Production Manager: Fred F. Pruss

Fat Quarters!
Jelly rolls!
Layer cakes!

Precut fabrics are so much fun, because one little bundle gives you a big variety of prints or solids. This means you can make scrap-style quilts—even if you don't have scraps! Pam McMahon's quilts stitch up beautifully with precuts such as fat quarters and jelly rolls. Add some additional yardage and make multi-fabric quilts that charm everyone who sees them!

meet the designer

Pam McMahon discovered her talent for patchwork about thirty years ago.

She says, "My passion for quilts began when my Grandmother Katie gave me the pieces of a Double Wedding Ring quilt that she started in the 1930s. Knowing that I enjoyed sewing, she suggested I might like to finish it. This was the start of my love for antique quilts and scrap quilts!

"In the late 1990s, I began working in a local quilt shop in Portland, Oregon. Soon, I was teaching beginning and intermediate quilting classes. I taught from some of my original designs, and the students encouraged me to write patterns for my quilts. In 2006, I relocated to Mesa, Arizona and decided to offer my patterns nationally. I like to create patterns that appeal to quilters of all skill levels. Typically, my designs use traditional blocks, and my preference is for traditional fabrics, but of course these quilts will look stunning in any precut fabrics you choose.

"Precuts make the process of quilt-making faster and more convenient. Plus, you have the instant benefit of a large group of coordinated fabrics. And what could be better than having a small piece of every fabric in the collections you love?"

To see more of Pam's fun quilts, visit PieceByPieceQuiltDesigns.com.

pinwheel palooza

Finished Quilt Size: 58" x 70" (147 cm x 178 cm)
Finished Block Size: 6" x 6" (15 cm x 15 cm)
Number of Blocks: 48

YARDAGE REQUIREMENTS

Yardage is based on 43"/44" (109 cm/112 cm) wide fabric with a usable width of 40" (102 cm). A fat eighth measures approximately 20" x 9" (51 cm x 23 cm).

An assortment of print fabric fat eighths. Pam used approximately 40 different prints.

An assortment of solid color fabric fat eighths. Pam used approximately 12 different solid colors.

$3^1/_8$ yds (2.9 m) of light print fabric for background

$1^1/_2$ yds (1.4 m) of fabric for outer border

$4^3/_8$ yds (4 m) of fabric for backing

$^5/_8$ yd (57 cm) of fabric for binding

You will also need:

66" x 78" (168 cm x 198 cm) piece of batting

CUTTING PIECES

Follow **Rotary Cutting**, page 56, to cut fabric. When cutting from yardage, cut all strips across the selvage-to-selvage width of the fabric. Borders include extra length for "insurance" and will be trimmed after assembling the quilt top center. All measurements include 1/4" seam allowances.

From the assortment of print fabric fat eighths:
- Cut 48 sets of 4 matching **rectangles** 2" x 3½" and 128 additional assorted rectangles 2" x 3½".

From the assortment of solid color fat eighths:
- Cut 48 sets of 8 matching **squares** 2" x 2".

From light print fabric for background:
- Cut 18 strips 3½"w. From these strips, cut 192 **background rectangles** 2" x 3½".
- Cut 6 spacer border strips 2"w.
- Cut 13 strips 2"w. From these strips, cut 256 **background squares** 2" x 2".

From fabric for outer border:
- Cut 7 **outer border strips** 6½"w.

From fabric for binding:
- Cut 7 **binding strips** 2½"w.

MAKING THE BLOCKS

Follow **Machine Piecing**, page 57, and **Pressing**, page 58.

1. For each Block, choose 4 matching print **rectangles** and 8 matching solid **squares**. Draw a diagonal line on wrong side of squares.
2. With right sides together, place 1 square on 1 end of 1 rectangle and stitch along drawn line. Trim ¼" from stitching line (**Fig. 1**). Open up (**Fig. 2**) and press.
3. Place another square on opposite end of rectangle. Stitch and trim as before (**Fig. 3**). Open up and press seam allowances toward triangle to make **Flying Geese A**. Make 4 Flying Geese A's.
4. Repeat Steps 1-3 using matching sets of rectangles and squares to make a total of 48 sets of 4 matching Flying Geese A's.

Fig. 1

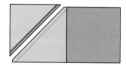

Fig. 2

Fig. 3

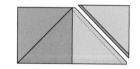

Flying Geese A
(make 4)

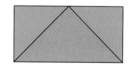

58" x 70" (147 cm x 178 cm)

5. Sew 1 **background rectangle** to each Flying Geese A to make **Unit 1**. Make 48 sets of 4 matching Unit 1's.
6. Sew 2 Unit 1's together to make **Unit 2**. Make 96 Unit 2's. Press seam allowances toward the Flying Geese Unit A.
7. Sew 2 Unit 2's together to make **Block**. Make 48 Blocks. Press seam allowances open to alleviate bulk in the center of the block.

ASSEMBLING THE QUILT TOP CENTER

1. With the open seam allowances running vertically and the remaining seam allowances opposing, sew 6 **Blocks** together to make a **Row**. Make 8 Rows. Press seam allowances to the left on odd numbered Rows and to the right on even numbered Rows.
2. Sew Rows together. When sewing rows together, the seam allowances between Blocks will be opposing and the seam allowances pressed open will need to be matched. Press seam allowances between rows toward the bottom of the quilt top.

Unit 1
(make 48 sets of 4)

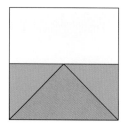

Unit 2 (make 96)

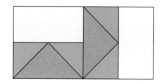

Block (make 48)

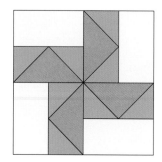

ADDING THE BORDERS

Adding the Spacer Borders

1. Sew **spacer border strips** together end to end using a diagonal seam (**Fig. 4**). Cut 2 **side spacer borders** 2" x $52^1/_2$" and 2 **top/bottom spacer borders** 2" x $43^1/_2$".
2. Refer to **Adding Squared Borders**, page 58, to add side, then top and bottom spacer borders to quilt top center.

Adding the Pieced Borders

1. Repeat **Making the Blocks**, page 6, Steps 1-3, using print **rectangles** and **background squares** to make 128 **Flying Geese B's**.
2. Sew 34 Flying Geese B's together to make **Side Border**. Make 2 Side Borders.
3. Sew the Side Borders to the quilt top. You might have to make border seams wider or narrower to adjust the length to fit the quilt top.
4. Sew 30 Flying Geese B's together to make **Top Border**. Repeat to make **Bottom Border**. Sew Top and Bottom Borders to quilt top.

Adding the Outer Borders

1. Sew **outer border strips** together end to end with a diagonal seam in same manner as previous. Cut 4 outer borders $6^1/_2$" x $61^1/_2$".
2. Refer to **Adding Squared Borders**, page 58, to add outer borders to quilt top. Press seam allowances toward the outer border.

COMPLETING THE QUILT

1. Follow **Quilting**, page 59, to mark, layer, and quilt as desired. Quilt shown is machine quilted in the center with an all-over meandering pattern. The outer borders are quilted with a flower and leaf pattern.
2. Follow **Making a Hanging Sleeve**, page 61, if a hanging sleeve is desired.
3. Sew **binding strips** together end to end using a diagonal seam (see **Fig. 4**) to make a continuous binding strip.
4. Follow **Attaching Binding**, page 62, to bind quilt.

Fig. 4

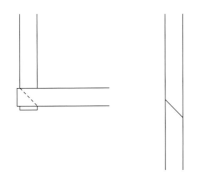

Flying Geese B
(make 128)

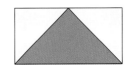

lickety-split

Finished Quilt Size: 61" x 61" (155 cm x 155 cm)
Finished Alternate Quilt Size: 61" x 77" (155 cm x 196 cm)
Finished Block Size: 8" x 8" (20 cm x 20 cm)
Number of Blocks: 16 [24]

Note: Instructions are written for the 61" x 61" quilt shown in the photo with an alternate size (61" x 77") in [ ]. Instructions will be easier to read if you circle all the numbers pertaining to your desired size quilt. If only one number is given, it applies to both sizes.

YARDAGE REQUIREMENTS

Yardage is based on 43"/44" (109 cm/112 cm) wide fabric with a usable width of 40" (102 cm). A layer cake includes 40 squares 10" x 10" (25 cm x 25 cm). The color names given in parenthesis indicate the color used in our quilt.

1 layer cake [45 squares 10" x 10"] **OR** more specifically:
- 9 [12] squares 10" x 10" of light and medium light print fabrics (cream)
- 10 [12] squares 10" x 10" of medium and medium dark print fabrics (gold, green)
- 8 [12] squares 10" x 10" of dark #1 print fabrics (black)
- 7 [9] squares 10" x 10" of dark #2 print fabrics (burgundy)

$^7/_8$ yd (80 cm) [1 yd (91 cm)] of fabric for inner borders (black)
$1^1/_2$ yds (1.4 m) [$1^5/_8$ yds (1.5 m)] of fabric for outer border (burgundy)
$3^7/_8$ yds (3.5 m) [$4^3/_4$ yds (4.3 m)] of fabric for backing
$^5/_8$ yd (57 cm) of fabric for binding

You will also need:
69" x 69" (175 cm x 175 cm) [69" x 85" (175 cm x 216 cm)] piece of batting

Note: When using precut pieces, include the outer points of the pinked edges in your measurement and for aligning the pieces for sewing.

CUTTING PIECES

Follow Rotary Cutting, page 56, to cut fabric. When cutting from yardage, cut all strips across the selvage-to-selvage width of the fabric. All measurements include $^1/_4$" seam allowances.

From light print squares (cream):
- For blocks, choose 4 [6] squares. Cut 2 strips $2^1/_2$"w from each square. Cut strips into 8 **squares** $2^1/_2$" x $2^1/_2$" for a *total* of 32 [48] squares.

From medium light print squares (cream):
- For blocks, choose 4 [6] squares. Cut 2 strips $2^1/_2$"w from each square. Cut strips into 8 **squares** $2^1/_2$" x $2^1/_2$" for a *total* of 32 [48] squares.

From medium print squares (gold):
- For blocks, choose 2 [3] squares. Cut 4 strips $2^1/_2$"w from each square. Cut strips into 16 **squares** $2^1/_2$" x $2^1/_2$" for a *total* of 32 [48] squares.

From medium dark print squares (green):
- For blocks, choose 4 [6] squares. Cut 4 strips $2^1/_2$"w from each square. Cut strips into 16 **squares** $2^1/_2$" x $2^1/_2$" for a *total* of 64 [96] squares.

From dark #1 print squares (black):
- For blocks, choose 4 [6] squares. Cut 2 strips $4^1/_2$"w from each square. Cut strips into 8 **rectangles** $2^1/_2$" x $4^1/_2$" for a *total* of 32 [48] rectangles.
- For blocks, use remaining 4 [6] squares and cut 2 strips $2^1/_2$"w from each square. Cut strips into 8 **squares** $2^1/_2$" x $2^1/_2$" for a *total* of 32 [48] squares.

From dark #2 print squares (burgundy):
- For blocks, choose 4 [6] squares. Cut 2 strips $4^1/_2$"w from each square. Cut strips into 8 **rectangles** $2^1/_2$" x $4^1/_2$" for a *total* of 32 [48] rectangles.

From remaining squares and partial squares (excluding dark #1):
- For checkerboard border, cut assorted squares $2^1/_2$" x $2^1/_2$" for a *total* of 160 [192] **squares**. Be sure to use a large variety of fabrics.

From fabric for inner borders (black):
- Cut 4 [5] **border #1 strips** $2^1/_2$"w.
- Cut 6 [7] **border #3 strips** $2^1/_2$"w.

From fabric for outer border (burgundy print):
- Cut 7 [8] **outer border strips** $6^1/_2$"w.

From fabric for binding:
- Cut 7 [8] **binding strips** $2^1/_2$"w.

61" x 61" (155 cm x 155 cm)

MAKING THE BLOCKS

*This quilt is made from 2 easy blocks. Notice that the only difference in the 2 blocks is the placement of the dark #1 and dark #2 fabrics. Follow **Machine Piecing**, page 57, and **Pressing**, page 58.*

1. Choose 32 [48] dark #1 print **rectangles** and 32 [48] light print **squares**. Draw a diagonal line on wrong side of squares.

2. With right sides together, place 1 square on 1 end of 1 rectangle and stitch along drawn line. Trim $^1/_4$" from stitching line (**Fig. 1**). Open up and press seam allowances toward triangle to make **Unit 1**. Make 32 [48] Unit 1's.

3. Repeat Steps 1-2 using 32 [48] dark #2 rectangles and 32 [48] dark #1 squares to make 32 [48] **Unit 2's**.

4. Sew 1 medium light print **square** to 1 medium dark print **square** to make **Unit 3**. Make 32 [48] Unit 3's. Press seam allowances toward medium dark square.

5. Sew 1 medium print **square** to 1 medium dark print **square** to make **Unit 4**. Make 32 [48] Unit 4's. Press seam allowances toward medium dark square.

6. Sew 1 **Unit 1** and 1 **Unit 4** together to make **Unit 5**. Make 16 [24] Unit 5's. Press the seam allowances toward Unit 1.

Fig. 1

Unit 1 (make 32 [48])

Unit 2
(make 32 [48])

Unit 3
(make 32 [48])

Unit 4 (make 32 [48])

Unit 5
(make 16 [24])

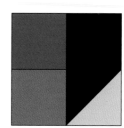

7. Sew 1 **Unit 2** and 1 **Unit 3** together to make **Unit 6**. Make 16 [24] Unit 6's. Press the seam allowances toward Unit 2.

8. Sew 2 **Unit 5's** and 2 **Unit 6's** together to make **Block A**. Make 8 [12] Block A's. Press seam allowances open. Block A's should measure $8^1/_2$" x $8^1/_2$" including seam allowances.

9. Sew 1 **Unit 2** and 1 **Unit 4** together to make **Unit 7**. Make 16 [24] Unit 7's. Press the seam allowances toward Unit 2.

10. Sew 1 **Unit 1** and 1 **Unit 3** together to make **Unit 8**. Make 16 [24] Unit 8's. Press the seam allowances toward Unit 1.

11. Sew 2 **Unit 7's** and 2 **Unit 8's** together to make **Block B**. Make 8 [12] Block B's. Press seam allowances open. Block B's should measure $8^1/_2$" x $8^1/_2$" including seam allowances.

ASSEMBLING THE QUILT TOP CENTER

Refer to photo, page 13, for 61" x 61" quilt and **Alternate Size Quilt Top Diagram**, *page 17, for 61" x 77" quilt.*

1. Beginning with Block A, sew 2 Block A's and 2 Block B's together to make **Row 1**. Make sure that pressed open seam allowances align. Press seam allowances between Blocks to the left. Make 2 [3] Row 1's.

2. Beginning with Block B, sew 2 Block B's and 2 Block A's together to make **Row 2**. Make sure that pressed open seam allowances align. Press seam allowances between Blocks to the right. Make 2 [3] Row 2's.

3. Sew Rows together to make quilt top center. Quilt top center should measure $32^1/_2$" x $32^1/_2$" [$32^1/_2$" x $48^1/_2$"] including seam allowances. When sewing rows together, the seam allowances between blocks will be opposing. Press seams between rows toward the bottom of the quilt top.

Unit 6
(make 16 [24])

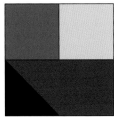

Block A
(make 8 [12])

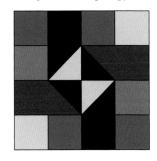

Unit 7
(make 16 [24])

Unit 8
(make 16 [24])

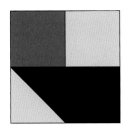

Block B
(make 8 [12])

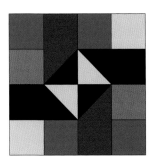

ADDING THE BORDERS

Adding Border #1
1. Sew **border #1 strips** together end to end using a diagonal seam (**Fig. 2**). Cut 2 **Side Border #1's** 2¹/₂" x 36¹/₂" [2¹/₂" x 52¹/₂"] and 2 **Top/Bottom Border #1's** 2¹/₂" x 40¹/₂".
2. Refer to **Adding Squared Borders**, page 58, to add **Side**, then **Top** and **Bottom Border #1's** to quilt top center.

Adding the Checkerboard Borders
1. Sew 2 squares together to make **Unit 9**. Make 80 [96] Unit 9's.
2. Alternating seam allowances, sew 2 assorted Unit 9's together to make 1 4-**Patch Unit**. Make 40 [48] 4-Patch Units.
3. Sew 9 [13] 4-Patch Units together to make **Side Checkerboard Border**. Press seam allowances to one side or open. Make 2 Side Checkerboard Borders.
4. Sew the Side Checkerboard Borders to the quilt top. You might have to make seams wider or narrower to adjust the length to fit the quilt top. Press the seam allowances towards Border #1.
5. Sew 11 4-Patch Units together to make **Top Checkerboard Border**. Press seam allowances to one side or open. Repeat to make **Bottom Checkerboard Border**.
6. Sew the Top and Bottom Checkerboard Borders to the quilt top. You might have to make seams wider or narrower to adjust the length to fit the quilt top. Press the seam allowances towards Border #1.

Adding Border #3
1. Sew **border #3 strips** together end to end using a diagonal seam (see **Fig. 2**). Cut 2 **Side Border #3's** 2¹/₂" x 48¹/₂" [2¹/₂" x 64¹/₂"] and 2 **Top/Bottom Border #3's** 2¹/₂" x 52¹/₂".
2. Sew **border #3's** to quilt top in same manner as previous. Press seam allowances toward the checkerboard border.

Adding Outer Border
1. Sew **outer border strips** together in same manner as previous. Cut 2 **Side Outer Borders** 6¹/₂" x 52¹/₂" [6¹/₂" x 68¹/₂"] and 2 **Top/Bottom Outer Borders** 6¹/₂" x 64¹/₂".
2. Sew **outer borders** to quilt top in same manner as previous. Press seam allowances toward Border #3.

Fig. 2

Unit 9
(make 80 [96])

4-Patch Unit
(make 40 [48])

TIP:

Pressing 4-Patch Units
Before pressing the final seam allowances, hold Unit on each side of the center seam and twist seam in opposite directions. The threads should "pop" where the seam crosses over other seams. If threads don't "pop," you can snip threads where they are sewn over. One seam will naturally want to lay "up" and the other will lay "down." Press seam allowances in opposite directions as shown in **Fig. 3**. A mini 4-Patch will be seen in the center of the Block; press. This alleviates the bulk in the center.

Fig. 3

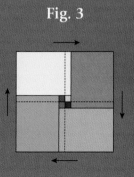

COMPLETING THE QUILT

1. Follow **Quilting**, page 59, to mark, layer, and quilt as desired. Quilt shown is machine quilted with an all-over swirl pattern.

2. Follow **Making a Hanging Sleeve**, page 61, if a hanging sleeve is desired.

3. Sew **binding strips** together end to end using a diagonal seam (see **Fig. 2**) to make a continuous binding strip.

4. Follow **Attaching Binding**, page 62, to bind quilt.

Alternate Size Quilt Top Diagram
61" x 77" (155 cm x 196 cm)

jelly jubilee

Finished Quilt Size: 49³/₈" x 57⁷/₈" (125 cm x 147 cm)
Finished Alternate Quilt Size: 57⁷/₈" x 74⁷/₈" (147 cm x 190 cm)
Finished Block Size: 6" x 6" (15 cm x 15 cm)
Number of Blocks: 32 [59]

Note: Instructions are written for the 49³/₈" x 57⁷/₈" quilt shown in the photo, page 21, with an alternate size, page 25, (57⁷/₈" x 74⁷/₈") in [ ]. Instructions will be easier to read if you circle all the numbers pertaining to your desired size quilt. If only one number is given, it applies to both sizes.

YARDAGE REQUIREMENTS

Yardage is based on 43"/44" (109 cm/112 cm) wide fabric with a usable width of 40" (102 cm). A jelly roll includes approximately 40 strips 2¹/₂" (6 cm) x width of fabric.

   1 jelly roll [2 jelly rolls]
   1¹/₈ yds (1 m) [1¹/₂ yds (1.4 m)] of light print fabric for setting
      triangles and background for pieced border
   1 yd (91 cm) [1¹/₈ yds (1 m)] of fabric for inner and outer borders
   3³/₄ yds (3.4 m) [4⁵/₈ yds (4.2 m)] of fabric for backing
   ¹/₂ yd (46 cm) [⁵/₈ yd (57 cm)] of fabric for binding
You will also need:
   58" x 66" (147 cm x 168 cm) [66" x 83" (168 cm x 211 cm)] piece
      of batting
   Omnigrid® 96L ruler **OR** Thangles™ 2" (5 cm) finished

CUTTING THE PIECES

*Follow **Rotary Cutting**, page 56, to cut fabric. When cutting from yardage, cut all strips across the selvage-to-selvage width of the fabric. All measurements include ¹/₄" seam allowances. Sort jelly roll strips into light prints and medium/dark prints. Each "set" is cut from 1 fabric.*

From assorted light print strips:
- For blocks, cut 32 [59] sets of 1 **rectangle** 2¹/₂" x 7" and 3 **squares** 2¹/₂" x 2¹/₂".

From medium/dark print strips:
- For blocks, cut 32 [59] sets of 1 **rectangle** 2¹/₂" x 7" and 2 **squares** 2¹/₂" x 2¹/₂".
- For pieced border, cut a total of 62 [80] **squares** 2¹/₂" x 2¹/₂". Use as many of the remaining strips as you like. Variety makes this border more interesting.

From light print fabric for setting triangles and background for pieced border:
- Cut 1 [2] strip(s) 9³/₄"w. From this (these) strip(s), cut 4 [5] squares 9³/₄" x 9³/₄". Cut each square diagonally *twice* for a total of 16 [20] **side setting triangles**. You will have 2 [0] left over.
- Cut 1 strip 5¹/₈"w. From this strip, cut 2 squares 5¹/₈" x 5¹/₈". Cut each square diagonally *once* for a total of 4 **corner setting triangles**.
- Cut 4 [5] strips 4¹/₈"w. From these strips, cut 30 [39] squares 4¹/₈" x 4¹/₈". Cut each square diagonally *twice* for a total of 120 [156] **large triangles**.
- Cut 1 strip 2³/₈"w. From this strip, cut 4 squares 2³/₈" x 2³/₈". Cut each square diagonally *once* for a total of 8 **small triangles**.

From fabric for borders:
- Cut 5 [6] **inner border strips** 1⁷/₈"w.
- Cut 6 [7] **outer border strips** 3¹/₂"w.

From fabric for binding:
- Cut 6 [8] **binding strips** 2¹/₂"w.

MAKING THE BLOCKS

*Follow **Machine Piecing**, page 57, and **Pressing**, page 58.*

Triangle-Squares

1.   From each set, you will use the 2¹/₂" x 7" rectangle to make Triangle-Squares. Matching right sides, place 1 light print **rectangle** on 1 medium/dark rectangle. Use either the Omnigrid 96L ruler or Thangles to make the triangle-squares.

Omnigrid Ruler:
Align the ruler on the rectangle with the dashed tip of the ruler on the top edge of the rectangle and 2" line at the bottom edge (**Fig. 1**). Cut the straight edge and the angled edge. Rotate the ruler and cut another set of triangles (**Fig. 2**). Cut a total of 4 sets of triangles. Sew triangles together along angled edge to complete **Triangle-Square**. Make 4 Triangle-Squares. Press seam allowances toward medium/dark print triangle.

Fig. 1

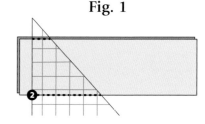

Fig. 2

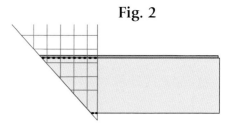

Continued on page 22.

$49^3/_8$" x $57^7/_8$" (125 cm x 147 cm)

Thangles:

Cut the Thangles strip into a section with 4 triangles. Pin the Thangles to the rectangles previously paired (**Fig. 3**). Use a short stitch length to sew on the dashed lines. After sewing, accurately cut triangles apart on solid lines to make 4 **Triangle-Squares** for every block. Remove paper according to manufacturer's instructions. Trim points from Triangle-Squares to eliminate bulk. Press seam allowances toward medium/dark print triangle.

2. Sew 1 medium/dark print **square**, 1 light print **square**, and 1 **Triangle-Square** together to make **Row 1**. Repeat to make **Row 3**. Press seam allowances away from Triangle-Square.

3. Sew 2 **Triangle-Squares** and 1 light print **square** together to make **Row 2**. Press seam allowances away from Triangle-Square.

4. Sew Rows 1-3 together to make **Block**. Block should measure $6^1/2$" x $6^1/2$" including seam allowances. Make 32 [59] Blocks.

ASSEMBLING THE QUILT TOP CENTER

*Refer to **Assembly Diagram**, page 24, for $49^3/8$" x $57^7/8$" quilt and **Alternate Size Quilt Top Diagram**, page 25, for $57^7/8$" x $74^7/8$" quilt.*

1. Rotating every other Block, sew Blocks and Setting Triangles together in diagonal Rows. Press seam allowances in direction indicated by arrows.

2. Sew Rows together to make Quilt Top Center. Seam allowances from Row to Row should be in opposing directions. Press long seams toward center of quilt top.

3. Making sure corners are at 90° angles, trim the quilt top center, allowing a $1/4$" seam allowance beyond the corners of each block.

ADDING THE INNER BORDERS

1. Sew **inner border strips** together end to end using a diagonal seam (**Fig. 4**). Cut 2 **side inner borders** $1^7/8$" x 47" [$1^7/8$" x 64"] **and 2 top/bottom inner borders** $1^7/8$" x $41^1/4$" [$1^7/8$" x $49^3/4$"].

2. Refer to **Adding Squared Borders**, page 58, to add side, then top and bottom inner borders to quilt top center.

3. Press the seam allowances toward the borders.

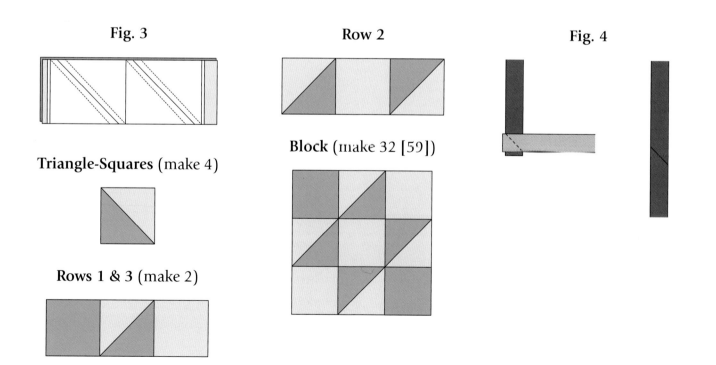

Fig. 3

Triangle-Squares (make 4)

Rows 1 & 3 (make 2)

Row 2

Block (make 32 [59])

Fig. 4

MAKING THE PIECED BORDERS

1. Sew 2 **large triangles** to 1 **square** to make **Unit 1**. Press seam allowances toward the square. Make 52 [70] Unit 1's.

2. Sew 2 **large triangles** to 1 **square** to make **Unit 2**. Press seam allowances toward the square. Make 2 Unit 2's.

3. Sew 1 **small triangle** and 1 **large triangle** to 1 **square** to make **Unit 3**. Press seam allowances toward the square. Make 2 Unit 3's.

4. Sew 1 **small triangle** and 1 **large triangle** to 1 **square** to make **Unit 4**. Press seam allowances toward the square. Make 2 Unit 4's.

5. Sew 2 **large triangles** and 1 **small triangle** to 1 **square** to make **Unit 5**. Press seam allowances toward the square. Make 4 Unit 5's.

6. Sew 14 [20] **Unit 1's**, 1 **Unit 3**, and 1 **Unit 4** together to make **Side Pieced Border**. Make 2 Side Pieced Borders. Press seam allowances in 1 direction.

7. Sew 12 [15] **Unit 1's** and 1 **Unit 2** together to make **Top Pieced Border**. Repeat to make **Bottom Pieced Border**. Press seam allowances in 1 direction.

Unit 1 (make 52, 70)

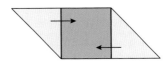

Unit 2 (make 2)

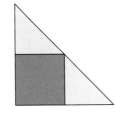

Unit 3 (make 2)

Unit 4 (make 2)

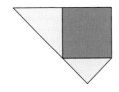

Unit 5 (make 4)

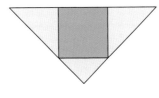

Side Pieced Border (make 2)

Alternate Size Side Pieced Border (make 2)

Top/Bottom Pieced Border (make 2)

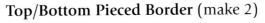

Alternate Size Top/Bottom Pieced Border (make 2)

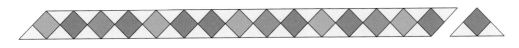

ADDING THE PIECED BORDERS

1. Sew the long side of the **Side Pieced Borders** to the quilt top. You might have to make seams wider or narrower to adjust the length to fit the quilt top.
2. Sew the long side of the **Top** and **Bottom Pieced Borders** to the quilt top. You might have to make seams wider or narrower to adjust the length to fit the quilt top.
3. Sew 1 **Unit 5** to each corner of quilt top.

ADDING THE OUTER BORDERS

1. Sew **outer border strips** together end to end using a diagonal seam (see **Fig. 4**, page 22) to make a continuous outer border. Cut 2 side outer borders $3^1/_2$" x $55^3/_8$" [$3^1/_2$" x $72^1/_2$"] and 2 top/bottom outer borders $3^1/_2$" x $52^7/_8$" [$3^1/_2$" x $61^1/_2$"].
2. Sew **side**, then **top** and **bottom outer borders** to quilt top center.
3. Press the seam allowances toward the borders.

Assembly Diagram
$49^3/_8$" x $57^7/_8$" (125 cm x 147 cm)

COMPLETING THE QUILT

1. Follow **Quilting**, page 59, to mark, layer, and quilt as desired. Quilt shown is machine quilted with feathered wreaths in each block, feathers in each setting triangle, and stipple quilting in the pieced border. There is also quilting in the ditch along each side of the inner border and channel quilting in the outer border.

2. Follow **Making a Hanging Sleeve**, page 61, if a hanging sleeve is desired.

3. Sew **binding strips** together end to end using a diagonal seam (see **Fig. 4**, page 22) to make a continuous binding strip.

4. Follow **Attaching Binding**, page 62, to bind quilt.

Alternate Size Quilt Top Diagram
57⁷/₈" x 74⁷/₈" (147 cm x 190 cm)

sew simple

Finished Quilt Size: $68^3/_8$" x $68^3/_8$" (174 cm x 174 cm)
Finished Alternate Quilt Size: 91" x 91" (231 cm x 231 cm)
Finished Block Sizes: 8" x 8" (20 cm x 20 cm) and 4" x 4" (10 cm x 10 cm)
Number of 16-Patch Blocks: 21 [49]
Number of 4-Patch Blocks: 40 [56]

Note: Instructions are written for the $68^3/_8$" x $68^3/_8$" quilt shown in the photo with an alternate size (91" x 91") in [ ]. Instructions will be easier to read if you circle all the numbers pertaining to your desired size quilt. If only one number is given, it applies to both sizes.

YARDAGE REQUIREMENTS
Yardage is based on 43"/44" (109 cm/112 cm) wide fabric with a usable width of 40" (102 cm). A jelly roll includes approximately 40 strips $2^1/_2$" (6 cm) x width of fabric.

- 1 jelly roll **OR** 36 medium/dark print strips $2^1/_2$"w and 1 light print strip $2^1/_2$"w [2 jelly rolls **OR** 65 medium/dark print strips $2^1/_2$"w and 2 light print strips $2^1/_2$"w]
- $2^1/_8$ yds (1.9 m) [$3^3/_8$ yds (3.1 m)] of light print fabric for alternate blocks, setting triangles, and background for pieced border
- $1^3/_8$ yds (1.3 m) [$1^3/_4$ yds (1.6 m)] of medium or dark print fabric for outer triangles and outer border
- $4^1/_4$ yds (3.9 m) [$8^1/_4$ yds (7.5 m)] of fabric for backing
- $^5/_8$ yd (57 cm) [$^7/_8$ yd (80 cm)] of fabric for binding

You will also need:
- $76^1/_2$" x $76^1/_2$" (194 cm x 194 cm) [99" x 99" (251 cm x 251 cm)] piece of batting

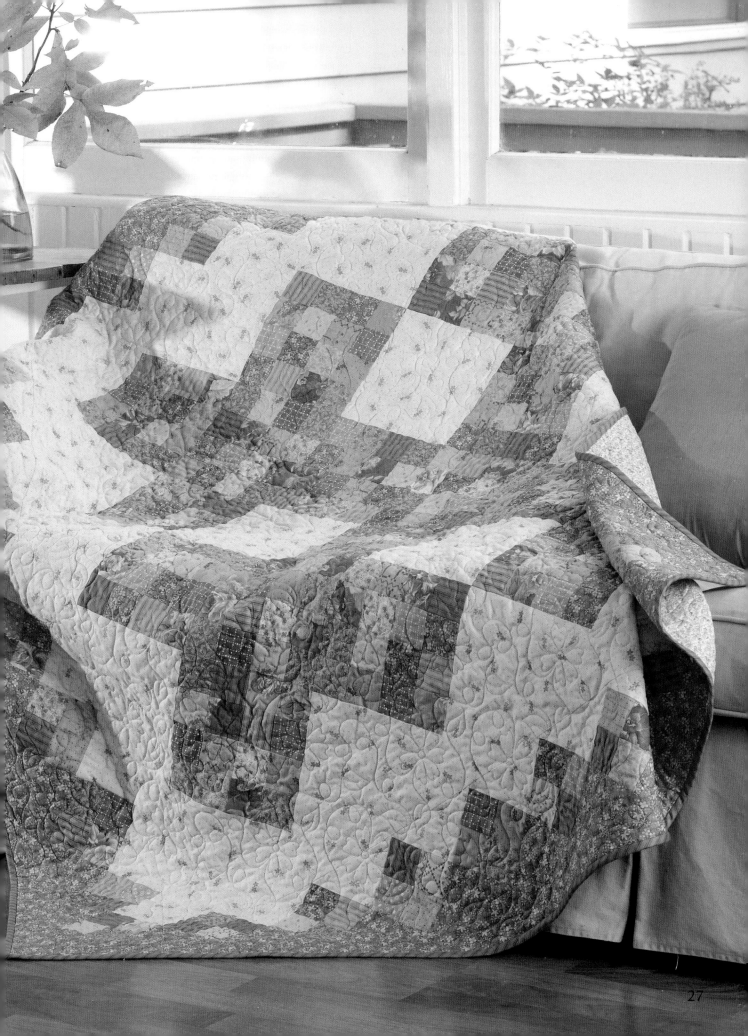

CUTTING THE PIECES

*Follow **Rotary Cutting**, page 56, to cut fabric. When cutting from yardage, cut all strips across the selvage-to-selvage width of the fabric. All measurements include ¹/₄" seam allowances.*

From light print strip(s):
- For 16-Patch Blocks, cut 1 [2] strip(s) in half to make 2 [4] **short strips** 20" long.

From medium and dark print strips:
- For 16-Patch Blocks, choose 25 [50] strips. Cut 5 [10] of these strips in half to make 10 [20] **short strips** 20" long. Set remaining **long strips** aside.
- For Pieced Border, choose 11 [15] strips. Cut strips in half to make 22 [30] **short strips** 20" long.

From light print fabric:
- Cut 1 [3] strip(s) 8¹/₂"w. From this (these) strip(s), cut 4 [12] **Alternate Blocks** 8¹/₂" x 8¹/₂".
- Cut 1 [2] strip(s) 13"w. From this (these) strip(s), cut 3 [5] squares 13" x 13". Cut each square diagonally *twice* for a total of 12 [20] **side setting triangles**.

- Cut 1 strip 7"w. From this strip, cut 2 squares 7" x 7". Cut each square diagonally *once* for a total of 4 **corner setting triangles**.
- Cut 6 [8] **inner border strips** 3³/₈"w.
- For pieced border, cut 2 [3] strips 7"w. From these strips, cut 8 [12] squares 7" x 7". Cut each square diagonally *twice* for a total of 32 [48] **large triangles**.
- For pieced border, cut 1 strip 3³/₄"w. From this strip, cut 6 squares 3³/₄" x 3³/₄". Cut each square diagonally *once* for a total of 12 **small triangles**.

From medium or dark print fabric:
- For pieced border, cut 2 [3] strips 7"w. From these strips, cut 8 [12] squares 7" x 7". Cut each square diagonally *twice* for a total of 32 [48] **large triangles**.
- For pieced border, cut 1 strip 3³/₄"w. From this strip, cut 10 squares 3³/₄" x 3³/₄". Cut each square diagonally *once* for a total of 20 **small triangles**.
- Cut 8 [10] **outer border strips** 3"w.

From fabric for binding:
- Cut 8 [10] **binding strips** 2¹/₂"w.

MAKING THE 16-PATCH BLOCKS

*Follow **Machine Piecing**, page 57, and **Pressing**, page 58.*

1. Sew 4 assorted **long strips** together to make **Strip Set A**. Press seam allowances to 1 side. Make 5 [10] Strip Set A's.
2. Sew 4 assorted **short strips** together to make **Strip Set B**. If using a light strip, do not position it on the outside edges. Press seam allowances to 1 side. Make 3 [6] Strip Set B's.

Strip Set A
(make 5 [10])

Strip Set B
(make 3 [6])

Continued on page 30.

$68^3/_8$" x $68^3/_8$" (174 cm x 174 cm)

3. Cut across Strip Set A's and Strip Set B's at $2^1/_2$" intervals to make approximately 104 [208] **Unit 1's.** This is more than needed to make 21 [49] Blocks but will ensure variety.

4. Sew 4 Unit 1's together to make a **16-Patch Block.** Make 21 [49] 16-Patch Blocks. You may have to "flip" seam allowances when sewing Unit 1's together to have opposing seams at all of the seam intersections. Press the final seam allowances in 1 direction.

ASSEMBLING THE QUILT TOP CENTER

Refer to photo, page 29, for $69^3/_8$" x $68^3/_8$" quilt and **Alternate Size Quilt Top Diagram,** *page 33, for 91" x 91" quilt.*

1. Sew 16-Patch Blocks, **Alternate Blocks,** and **side setting triangles** together in diagonal Rows. Press seam allowances toward the Alternate Blocks and the Side Setting Triangles. Sew 1 **corner setting triangle** to each corner of quilt top center. Press seam allowances between Rows toward the bottom of the quilt top.

2. Making sure corners are at 90° angles, trim the quilt top center, allowing a $1/_4$" seam allowance beyond the corners of each block.

ADDING THE INNER BORDERS

1. Sew **inner border strips** together end to end using a diagonal seam (**Fig. 1**) to make a continuous border strip. Cut 2 **side inner borders** $3^3/_8$" x $49^3/_4$" [$3^3/_8$" x $72^3/_8$"] **and** 2 **top/bottom inner borders** $3^3/_8$" x $55^1/_2$" [$3^3/_8$" x $78^1/_8$"].

2. Refer to **Adding Squared Borders,** page 58, to add **side,** then **top** and **bottom inner borders** to quilt top center.

3. Press the seam allowances toward the borders.

Strip Sets A & B

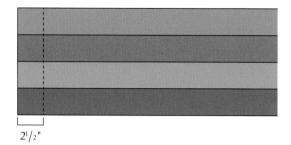

$2^1/_2$"

Unit 1
(make 104 [208])

16-Patch Block (make 21 [49])

Fig. 1

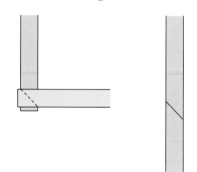

MAKING THE 4-PATCH BLOCKS

1. Sew 2 assorted **short strips** together to make **Strip Set C**. Press seam allowances to 1 side. Make 11 [15] Strip Set C's.

2. Cut across each Strip Set C at 2½" intervals to make approximately 88 [120] Units 2's. This is more than needed to make 40 [56] Blocks but will ensure variety.

3. Sew 2 Unit 2's together to make a 4-**Patch Block**. Make 40 [56] 4-Patch Blocks. You may have to "flip" seam allowances when sewing Unit 2's together to have opposing seams at the seam intersections. Before pressing the final seam allowances, hold Unit on each side of the center seam and twist seam in opposite directions. The threads should "pop" where the seam crosses over other seams. If threads don't "pop," you can snip threads where they are sewn over. One seam will naturally want to lay "up" and the other will lay "down" (**Fig. 2**). A mini 4-Patch will be seen in the center of the block; press. This alleviates the bulk in the intersection.

Strip Set C
(make 11 [15])

2½"

Unit 2
(make 88 [120])

4-Patch Block (make 40, 56)

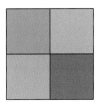

Fig. 2

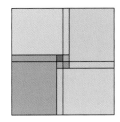

MAKING THE PIECED BORDER

1. Sew 1 light **large triangle**, 1 medium/dark **large triangle**, and 1 4-**Patch Block** together to make **Unit 2**. Make 28 [44] Unit 2's.

2. Sew 1 light **small triangle**, 1 medium/dark **small triangle**, 1 medium/dark **large triangle**, and 1 4-**Patch Block** together to make **Unit 3**. Make 4 Unit 3's.

3. Sew 1 light **small triangle**, 1 medium/dark **small triangle**, 1 light **large triangle**, and 1 4-**Patch Block** together to make **Unit 4**. Make 4 Unit 4's.

4. Sew 1 light **small triangle**, 3 medium/dark **small triangles**, and 1 4-**Patch Block** together to make **Unit 5**. Make 4 Unit 5's.

5. Sew 1 **Unit 4**, 7 [11] **Unit 2's**, and 1 **Unit 3** together to make **Side Pieced Border**. Make 2 Side Pieced Borders.

6. Sew 2 **Unit 5's**, 1 **Unit 4**, 7 [11] **Unit 2's**, and 1 **Unit 3** together to make **Top Pieced Border**. Repeat to make **Bottom Pieced Border**.

ADDING THE PIECED BORDERS

1. Sew the **Side Pieced Borders** to the quilt top. You might have to make seams wider or narrower to adjust the length to fit the quilt top.

2. Sew the **Top** and **Bottom Pieced Borders** to the quilt top. You might have to make seams wider or narrower to adjust the length to fit the quilt top.

Unit 2 (make 28 [44])

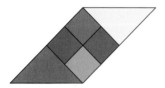

Unit 3 (make 4)

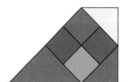

Unit 4 (make 4)

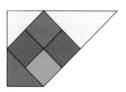

Unit 5 (make 4)

Side Pieced Border (make 2)

Small Quilt

Top/Bottom Pieced Border (make 2)

Small Quilt

Side Pieced Border (make 2)

Large Quilt

Top/Bottom Pieced Border (make 2)

Large Quilt

ADDING THE OUTER BORDERS

1. Sew **outer border strips** together end to end using a diagonal seam (see **Fig. 1**, page 30). Cut 2 side outer borders 3" x 66$^7/_8$" [3" x 89$^1/_2$"] and 2 top/bottom outer borders 3" x 71$^7/_8$" [3" x 94$^1/_2$"].
2. Refer to **Adding Squared Borders**, page 58, to add **side**, then **top** and **bottom outer borders** to quilt top center. Press the seam allowances toward the borders.

COMPLETING THE QUILT

1. Follow **Quilting**, page 59, to mark, layer, and quilt as desired. Quilt shown is machine quilted with an all-over swirl pattern.
2. Follow **Making a Hanging Sleeve**, page 61, if a hanging sleeve is desired.
3. Sew **binding strips** together end to end using a diagonal seam (see **Fig. 1**, page 30) to make a continuous binding strip.
4. Follow **Attaching Binding**, page 62, to bind quilt.

Alternate Size Quilt Top Diagram
91" x 91" (231 cm x 231 cm)

light & breezy

Finished Quilt Size: $53^1/_2$" x $69^1/_2$" (136 cm x 177 cm)
Finished Block Size: 8" x 8" (20 cm x 20 cm)
Number of Blocks: 18 Star Blocks and 17 Alternate Blocks

YARDAGE REQUIREMENTS

Yardage is based on 43"/44" (109 cm/112 cm) wide fabric with a usable width of 40" (102 cm). A jelly roll includes approximately 40 strips $2^1/_2$" (6 cm) x width of fabric. A layer cake includes 40 squares 10" x 10" (25 cm x 25 cm). The color names given in parenthesis indicate the color used on our quilt.

1 jelly roll and 1 layer cake **OR** if you choose to use yardage the following is needed:
- $1^3/_8$ yds (1.3 m) *total* of assorted light prints for Star Block backgrounds and Alternate Block corners (creams).
- $^3/_8$ yd (34 cm) *total* of assorted medium light prints for Star Block pinwheels (pinks, blues)
- $^3/_4$ yd (69 cm) *total* of assorted medium prints for Alternate Block rectangles (blues)
- $^3/_4$ yd (69 cm) *total* of assorted medium dark prints for Star Blocks (greys, corals, dark pinks)
- $^3/_4$ yd (69 cm) *total* of assorted dark prints for Star Blocks (corals, greys)
- $^1/_2$ yd (46 cm) *total* of assorted dark prints for Alternate Blocks (grey)

$^3/_8$ yd (34 cm) of print fabric for inner border and flange
$1^1/_2$ yds (1.4 m) of print fabric for outer border
$4^3/_8$ yds (4 m) of fabric for backing
$^5/_8$ yd (57 cm) of fabric for binding

You will also need:
$61^1/_2$" x $77^1/_2$" (156 cm x 197 cm) piece of batting
Omnigrid® 96L ruler

Note: When using precut pieces, include the outer points of the pinked edges in your measurement and for aligning the pieces for sewing.

CUTTING THE PIECES

*Follow **Rotary Cutting**, page 56, to cut fabric. Cut from the Jelly Roll first except when cutting the dark $4^1/2$" x $4^1/2$" squares. Each "set" should be cut from 1 fabric. When cutting from yardage, cut all strips across the selvage-to-selvage width of the fabric. All measurements include $1/4$" seam allowances.*

For Star Blocks
From light print strips (creams):
- For backgrounds, cut 18 sets of 4 **large rectangles** $2^1/2$" x $4^1/2$" and 2 **small rectangles** $2^1/2$" x $3^1/2$".

From medium light print strips (pinks, blues):
- Cut 18 sets of 2 matching **small rectangles** $2^1/2$" x $3^1/2$".

From medium dark print strips (greys, corals, dark pinks):
- Cut 18 sets of 2 matching **small rectangles** $2^1/2$" x $3^1/2$".
- Cut 18 sets of 4 matching **small squares** $2^1/2$" x $2^1/2$".

From dark print strips (corals, greys):
- Cut 18 sets of 4 matching **small squares** $2^1/2$" x $2^1/2$".
- Cut 18 sets of 2 matching **small rectangles** $2^1/2$" x $3^1/2$".

For Alternate Blocks
From light print strips (creams):
- Cut 17 sets of 4 matching **small squares** $2^1/2$" x $2^1/2$".

From medium print strips (blues):
- Cut 17 sets of 4 matching **large rectangles** $2^1/2$" x $4^1/2$".

From dark print layer cakes (greys):
- Cut a *total* of 17 **large squares** $4^1/2$" x $4^1/2$".

For Borders
From fabric for inner border and flange:
- Cut 6 **inner border strips** $3/4$"w.
- Cut 7 **flange strips** 1"w.

From fabric for outer border:
- Cut 7 **outer border strips** $6^1/2$"w.

For Binding
From fabric for binding:
- Cut 7 **binding strips** $2^1/2$"w.

MAKING THE BLOCKS

*Follow **Machine Piecing**, page 57, and **Pressing**, page 58.*

1. Matching right sides, place 1 medium light print **small rectangle** on 1 medium dark **small rectangle**. Align the ruler on the small rectangles with the dashed tip of the ruler on the top edge of the rectangle and 2" line at the bottom edge (**Fig. 1**). Cut the straight edge and the angled edge. Rotate the ruler and cut another set of triangles (**Fig. 2**). Sew triangles together along angled edge to complete **Triangle-Square A**. Make 18 sets of 4 matching Triangle-Square A's. Press seam allowances toward dark print triangle.

Fig. 1   Fig. 2

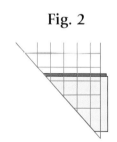

Triangle-Square A
(make 18 sets of 4 matching)

$53^1/_2$" x $69^1/_2$" (136 cm x 177 cm)

Fig. 3

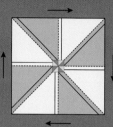

2. Sew 4 matching **Triangle-Square A's** together to make 1 **Pinwheel Unit**. Make 18 Pinwheel Units.

3. Repeat Step 1 using light print small rectangles and dark print small rectangles to make 18 sets of 4 matching **Triangle-Square B's**.

4. Choose 4 matching light print **large rectangles** (same as Triangle-Square B's), 4 matching dark print **small squares**, and 4 matching medium dark print **small squares** (same as the Pinwheel Units). Draw a diagonal line on wrong side of small squares.

5. With right sides together, place 1 dark small square on left end of 1 rectangle and stitch along drawn line. Trim ¹/₄" from stitching line (**Fig. 3**). Open up and press seam allowances toward small triangle (**Fig. 4**).

6. Place medium dark print small square on right end of rectangle. Stitch and trim as previous. Open up and press seam allowances toward triangle to make **Flying Geese**. Flying Geese should measure 2¹/₂" x 4¹/₂" including seam allowances. Make a total of 18 sets of 4 matching Flying Geese.

Pinwheel Unit
(make 18)

Triangle-Square B
(make 18 sets of 4 matching)

Fig. 3

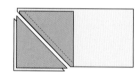

Fig. 4

Flying Geese
(make 18 sets of 4 matching)

Star Block

1. For each Block, choose 4 matching Flying Geese and 4 matching Triangle-Square B's with the same light print. Choose 1 Pinwheel Unit with the same medium dark print as in the Flying Geese.
2. Sew 2 **Triangle-Square B's** and 1 **Flying Geese** together to make **Row 1**. Make 2 Row 1's.
3. Sew 2 **Flying Geese** and 1 **Pinwheel Unit** together to make **Row 2**.
4. Sew **Row 1's** and **Row 2** together to make **Star Block**. Star Block should measure $8^1/_2$" x $8^1/_2$" including seam allowances. Make 18 Star Blocks.

Alternate Block

1. Choose 1 dark print **large square**, 4 matching medium print (blue) **large rectangles**, and 4 matching light print **small squares**.
2. Sew 2 light print **small squares** and 1 medium print **large rectangle** together to make **Row 1**. Press seam allowances toward large rectangle. Make 2 Row 1's.
3. Sew 2 medium print **large rectangles** and 1 dark print **large square** together to make **Row 2**. Press seam allowances toward large rectangles.
4. Sew **Row 1's** and **Row 2** together to make **Alternate Block**. Alternate Block should measure $8^1/_2$" x $8^1/_2$" including seam allowances. Make 17 Alternate Blocks.

ASSEMBLING THE QUILT TOP CENTER

*Refer to **Quilt Top Diagram**, page 46.*

1. Beginning with a Star Block and alternating Blocks, sew 3 Star Blocks and 2 Alternate Blocks together to make **Row 1**. Press seam allowances toward the Alternate Blocks. Make 4 Row 1's.
2. Beginning with an Alternate Block and alternating Blocks, sew 3 Alternate Blocks and 2 Star Blocks together to make **Row 2**. Press seam allowances toward the Alternate Blocks. Make 3 Row 2's.
3. Sew Row 1's and Row 2's together to make quilt top center. Press the seam allowances between rows toward the bottom of the quilt top center.

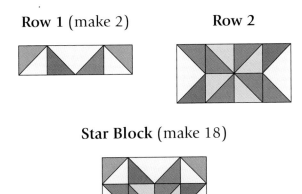

Row 1 (make 2)   Row 2

Star Block (make 18)

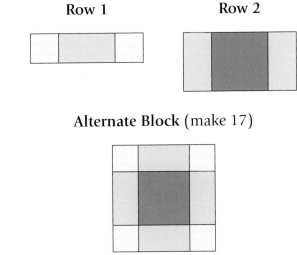

Row 1   Row 2

Alternate Block (make 17)

ADDING THE BORDERS

1. Sew **inner border strips** together end to end using a diagonal seam (**Fig. 5**). Cut 2 **side inner borders** $^3/_4$" x $60^1/_2$" and 2 **top/bottom borders** $^3/_4$" x $44^1/_2$".

2. Refer to **Adding Squared Borders**, page 58, to sew **side**, then **top** and **bottom inner borders** to quilt top center. Press the seam allowances toward the borders.

3. Repeat Steps 1-2 and use **outer border strips** to add the outer borders. Cut 2 **side outer borders** $6^1/_2$" x 61" and 2 **top/bottom outer borders** $6^1/_2$" x 57".

COMPLETING THE QUILT

1. Follow **Quilting**, page 59, to mark, layer, and quilt as desired. Quilt shown is machine quilted with an all-over swirl pattern.

2. Sew **flange strips** together end to end using a diagonal seam (see **Fig. 5**) to make a continuous flange strip. Cut 2 side flange strips 1" x 73" and 2 top/bottom flange strips 1" x 57".

3. Refer to **Adding Squared Borders**, page 58, to measure and trim flange strips to length.

4. Matching *wrong* sides, press each flange strip in half lengthwise.

5. Matching right sides and raw edges, sew a side flange strip to each side of quilt top. Repeat with top and bottom flange strips, overlapping side flange strips at corners.

6. Follow **Making a Hanging Sleeve**, page 61, if a hanging sleeve is desired.

7. Sew **binding strips** together end to end using a diagonal seam (see **Fig. 5**) to make a continuous binding strip.

8. Follow **Attaching Binding**, page 62, to bind quilt.

Fig. 5

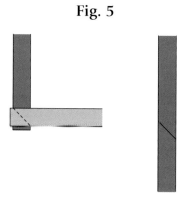

Quilt Top Diagram

hem 'n' haws

Finished Quilt Size: 60$\frac{1}{2}$" x 70$\frac{1}{2}$" (154 cm x 179 cm)
Finished Alternate Quilt Size: 70$\frac{1}{2}$" x 90$\frac{1}{4}$" (179 cm x 229 cm)
Finished Block Size: 6" x 6" (15 cm x 15 cm)
Number of Blocks: 30 Block A's and 20 Block B's [48 Block A's and 35 Block B's]

Note: Instructions are written for the 60$\frac{1}{2}$" x 70$\frac{1}{2}$" quilt shown in the photo, page 45, with an alternate size, page 49 (70$\frac{1}{2}$" x 90$\frac{1}{4}$") in [ ]. Instructions will be easier to read if you circle all the numbers pertaining to your desired size quilt. If only one number is given, it applies to both sizes. The color names given in parenthesis indicate the color used on our quilt.

YARDAGE REQUIREMENTS

Yardage is based on 43"/44" (109 cm/112 cm) wide fabric with a usable width of 40" (102 cm). A jelly roll includes approximately 40 strips 2$\frac{1}{2}$" (6 cm) x width of fabric.

   1 jelly roll [2 jelly rolls] for Block A's and B's
   $\frac{5}{8}$ yd (57 cm) [1$\frac{1}{8}$ yds (1 m)] of light print fabric for Block B's
   1 yd (91 cm) [1$\frac{5}{8}$ yds (1.5 m)] of medium light print fabric for
     sashings
   $\frac{1}{4}$ yd (23 cm) of fabric for cornerstones (black)
   1 yd (91 cm) of fabric for setting triangles (red)
   2$\frac{5}{8}$ yds (2.4 m) [3$\frac{3}{8}$ yds (3.1 m)] of fabric for border*
   4$\frac{1}{2}$ yds (4.1 m) [5$\frac{1}{2}$ yds (5 m)] of fabric for backing
   $\frac{5}{8}$ yd (57 cm) [$\frac{3}{4}$ yd (69 cm)] of fabric for binding
You will also need:
   68$\frac{1}{2}$" x 78$\frac{1}{2}$" (174 cm x 199 cm) [78$\frac{1}{2}$" x 98$\frac{1}{4}$" (199 cm x 250 cm)]
     piece of batting

*If fabric is not directional, all borders can be cut lengthwise and only
   1$\frac{7}{8}$ yds (1.7 m) [2$\frac{5}{8}$ yds (2.4 m)] will be needed.

CUTTING THE PIECES

*Follow **Rotary Cutting**, page 56, to cut fabric. When cutting from yardage, cut all strips across the selvage-to-selvage width of the fabric. All measurements include ¹/₄" seam allowances.*

From 8 [12] light print strips (ivory):
- For blocks, cut each strip into 2¹/₂" x 2¹/₂" **squares** for a *total* of 120 [192] squares.

From 15 [24] medium print strips (blue):
- For blocks, cut each strip into 2¹/₂" x 4¹/₂" **rectangles** for a *total* of 120 [192] rectangles.

From 7 [11] medium dark print strips (red):
- For blocks, cut each strip into 2¹/₂" x 2¹/₂" **squares** for a *total* of 100 [166] squares.

From 7 [12] dark print strips (black):
- For blocks, cut each strip into 2¹/₂" x 2¹/₂" **squares** for a *total* of 110 [179] squares.

From light print fabric:
- For Block B's, cut 5 [9] strips 2¹/₂"w. From these strips, cut a *total* of 40 [70] **rectangles** 2¹/₂" x 4¹/₂" .
- For Block B's, cut 3 [5] strips 2¹/₂"w. From these strips, cut each strip into 2¹/₂" x 2¹/₂" **squares** for a *total* of 40 [70] squares.

From medium light print fabric for sashings:
- Cut 5 [8] **strips** 6¹/₂"w. From these strips, cut 120 [192] **sashings** 1¹/₂" x 6¹/₂".

From fabric for cornerstones (black):
- Cut 3 [5] strips 1¹/₂"w. From these strips, cut 71 [110] **cornerstones** 1¹/₂" x 1¹/₂".

From fabric for setting triangles (red):
- Cut 2 strips 12"w. From these strips, cut 5, [6] squares 12" x 12". Cut each square diagonally *twice* to make 20 [24] **setting triangles**. You will use 18 [24] and have 2 [0] left over. These are cut oversized.
- Cut 1 strip 8"w. From this strip, cut 2 squares 8" x 8". Cut each square diagonally *once* to make 4 **corner setting triangles**. These are cut oversized.

From fabric for borders:
- Cut 2 *lengthwise* side borders 5¹/₂" x 64" [5¹/₂" x 83³/₄"].
- Cut 2 *crosswise* top/bottom borders 5¹/₂" x 64" [5¹/₂" x 74"], pieced as needed.

From fabric for binding:
- Cut 8 [9] binding strips 2¹/₂"w.

MAKING THE BLOCKS

*Follow **Machine Piecing**, page 57, and **Pressing**, page 58.*

Block A

1. For Flying Geese Unit A's, choose 60 [96] medium print (blue) **rectangles**, 60 [96] dark print (black) **squares**, and 60 [96] light print (ivory) **squares**.

2. Draw a diagonal line on wrong side of squares. With right sides together, place 1 dark print (black) square on the left end of 1 medium print (blue) rectangle and stitch along drawn line. Trim ¹/₄" from stitching line (**Fig. 1**). Open up and press seam allowances toward triangle to make **Unit 1**. Make 60 [96] Unit 1's.

Fig. 1

Unit 1 (make 60 [96])

$60^{1}/_{2}$" x $70^{1}/_{2}$" (154 cm x 179 cm)

3. Repeat Step 2 using 1 light print (ivory) square on right end of rectangle to make 60 [96] **Flying Geese Unit A's**.

4. Repeat Step 2, using the remaining 60 [96] medium print (blue) rectangles, 60 [96] medium dark print (red) squares, and 60 [96] light print (ivory) squares to make 60 [96] **Flying Geese Unit B's**.

5. Refer to **Block A Assembly Diagram**, to sew 2 **Flying Geese Unit A's**, 2 **Flying Geese Unit B's**, and 1 dark print (black) **square** together to make **Block A**. When sewing seam #1, sew only about half of the seam (from dot to dot). Finish the partial seam last, sewing from the outer edge to meet and overlap seam #1 a few stitches. Press seam allowances toward Flying Geese Units. Block A should measure 6^1/$_2$" x 6^1/$_2$" including seam allowances. Make 30 [48] Block A's.

Block B

1. For Block B's, choose 40 [70] light print **rectangles**, 40 [70] light print **squares**, 40 [70] medium dark print (red) **squares**, and 20 [35] dark print (black) **squares**.

2. Sew 1 light print **rectangle** and 1 medium dark print (red) **square** together to make **Unit 2**. Make 40 [70] Unit 2's. Press the seam allowances toward the medium dark print (red) square.

3. Sew 2 light print **squares** and 1 dark print (black) **square** together to make **Unit 3**. Make 20 [35] Unit 3's. Press the seam allowances toward dark print square.

4. Sew 2 **Unit 2's** and 1 **Unit 3** together to make **Block B**. Press the seam allowances away from the center. Block B's should measure 6^1/$_2$" x 6^1/$_2$" including seam allowances. Make 20 [35] Block B's.

Flying Geese Unit A
(make 60 [96])

Flying Geese Unit B
(make 60 [96])

Unit 2 (make 40 [70])

Unit 3 (make 20 [35])

Block A Assembly Diagram
(make 30 [48])

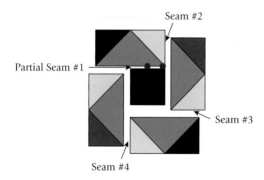

Block B (make 20 [35])

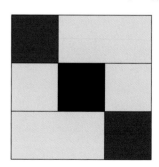

ASSEMBLING THE QUILT TOP CENTER

*Refer to **Assembly Diagram**, page 48. The setting triangles, corner setting triangles, and outer cornerstones are cut oversized and will be trimmed after quilt top center is assembled.*

1.   Sew **cornerstones** and **sashings** together to make **Sashing Rows** (odd number rows on Assembly Diagram). Press all seam allowances toward sashings.
2.   Alternating blocks, sew sashings and blocks together to make **Block Rows** (even number rows). Press all seam allowances toward sashings.
3.   Sew Sashing Row 1 and Block Row 2 together, then add 2 **side setting triangles**.
4.   Continue sewing Rows (3 & 4, 5 & 6, 7 & 8) together in this manner. Rows 9 & 10 should be sewn in the same manner, however you will only use 1 side setting triangle.
     Row 11 should be sewn to the 9/10 section. Rows 12 & 13 will be sewn together the same as 9 & 10. **Do not** add the corner setting triangles at this time.
5.   Starting at the opposite corner, sew the remainder of the Rows together in the same manner.
6.   Sew the 2 halves of the quilt top center together.
7.   Sew the **corner setting triangles** to the corners of the quilt top center.
8.   Making sure the corners are at 90° angles, trim the quilt top center, allowing a $^1/_4$" seam allowance beyond the corners of each of the sashings.

ADDING THE BORDER

1.   Refer to **Adding Squared Borders**, page 58, to add side, then top and bottom **borders** to quilt top center.
2.   Press the seam allowances toward the borders.

COMPLETING THE QUILT

1.   Follow **Quilting**, page 59, to mark, layer, and quilt as desired. Quilt shown is machine quilted with swirls in the Flying Geese sections of each Block A, 4 petals in each Block B, a squiggly line in each sashing, a freehand petal pattern in each setting triangle, and feathers in the border.
2.   Follow **Making a Hanging Sleeve**, page 61, if a hanging sleeve is desired.
3.   Sew **binding strips** together end to end using a diagonal seam (**Fig. 2**) to make a continuous binding strip.
4.   Follow **Attaching Binding**, page 62, to bind quilt.

Fig. 2

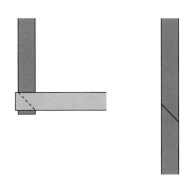

Assembly Diagram
$60^1/_2$" x $70^1/_2$" (154 cm x 179 cm)

Corner

Row 1

Row 2

Row 3

Row 4

Row 5

Row 6

Row 7

Row 8

Row 9

Row 10

Row 11

Row 12

Row 13

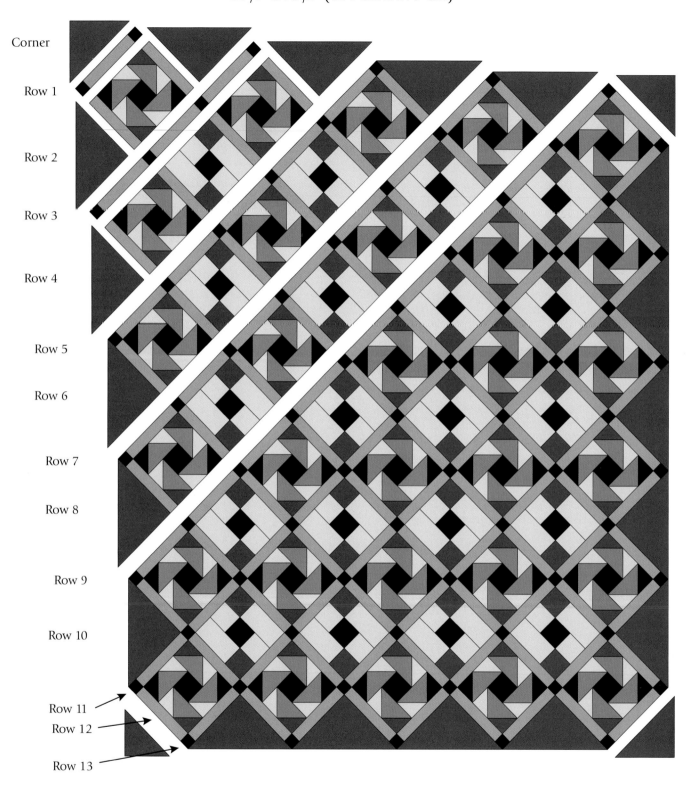

Alternate Size Quilt Top Diagram
70^1/$_2$" x 90^1/$_4$" (179 cm x 229 cm)

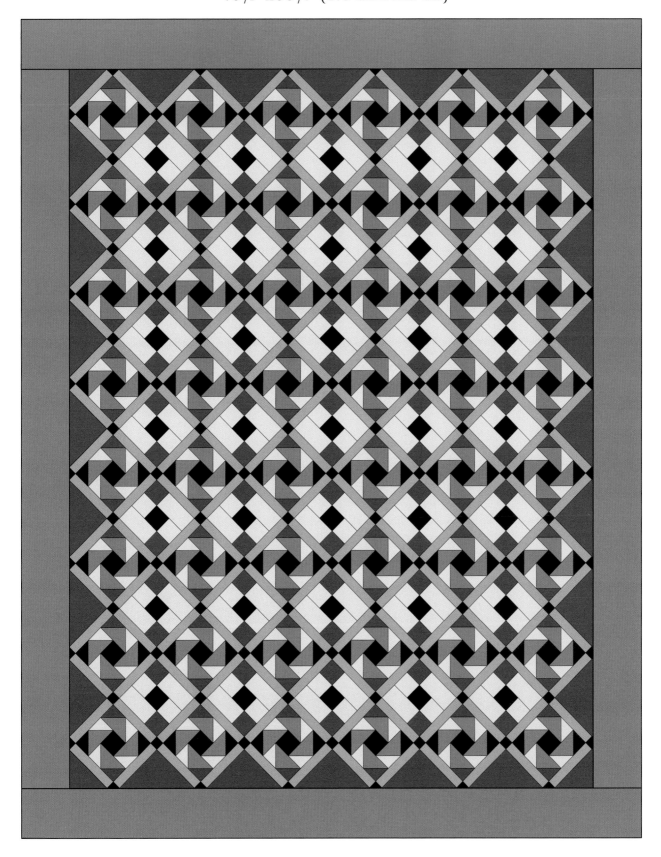

double dare ya!

Finished Quilt Size: 52" x 64³/₄" (132 cm x 164 cm)
Finished Block Size: 12" x 12" (30 cm x 30 cm)
Number of Blocks: 12

YARDAGE REQUIREMENTS
Yardage is based on 43"/44" (109 cm/112 cm) wide fabric with a usable width of 40" (102 cm). A jelly roll includes approximately 40 strips 2¹/₂" (6 cm) x width of fabric. The color names given in parenthesis indicate the color used on our quilt.

   2 jelly rolls or 80 strips 2¹/₂" wide – The 2 rolls of strips should
     include at least 18 lights and a variety of mediums and darks
   ¹/₂ yd (46 cm) of medium dark fabric for sashings
   ⁵/₈ yd (57 cm) of dark fabric for sashing squares and binding
     (black solid)
   4¹/₈ yds (3.8 m) of fabric for backing
You will also need:
   60" x 73" (152 cm x 185 cm) piece of batting

CUTTING PIECES

*Follow **Rotary Cutting**, page 56, to cut fabric. When cutting from yardage, cut all strips across the selvage-to-selvage width of the fabric. All measurements include $1/4$" seam allowances.*

From assorted light print strips (beige):
- Cut 192 **squares (A)** $2^1/2$" x $2^1/2$" for Flying Geese Unit A's and Triangle-Squares.
- Cut 34 **border #1 rectangles** $2^1/2$" x $6^1/2$".

From assorted medium dark print strips (green):
- Cut 12 sets of 4 matching **corner squares (B)** $2^1/2$" x $2^1/2$".

From assorted medium dark print strips:
- Cut 12 sets of 4 matching **rectangles (F)** $2^1/2$" x $4^1/2$" for Flying Geese Unit B's.

From assorted dark or medium dark print strips:
- Choose 12 assorted strips for the on-point frame in the block. From each strip:
  - Cut 1 set of 4 **rectangles (E)** $2^1/2$" x $4^1/2$" and 8 **squares (H)** $2^1/2$" x $2^1/2$".
- Cut 24 **squares (G)** $2^1/2$" x $2^1/2$" for Four-Patch Units (assorted color prints). You can use 2 from the same print or 2 from different prints; just use the same color fabric.

- Cut 12 sets of 4 matching **accent squares (D)** $2^1/2$" x $2^1/2$" (assorted color prints).
- For borders, cut a variety of strips $2^1/2$"w and ranging from $6^1/2$" to 10" long.
  - For border #2, cut enough **rectangles** to *total* at least 212" when sewn together.
  - For border #3, cut enough **rectangles** to *total* at least 230" when sewn together.

From assorted dark print strips (black):
- Cut 96 **squares (C)** $2^1/2$" x $2^1/2$" for Triangle-Squares.
- Cut 24 **squares (G)** $2^1/2$" x $2^1/2$" for Four-Patch Units.

From fabric for sashings:
- Cut 11 strips $1^1/4$"w. From these strips, cut 31 **sashing strips** $1^1/4$" x $12^1/2$".

From fabric for sashing squares and binding (black solid):
- Cut 5 squares $2^1/2$" x $2^1/2$". Cut each square into 4 **sashing squares** $1^1/4$" x $1^1/4$" for a total of 20 sashing squares.
- Cut 7 **binding strips** $2^1/2$"w.

MAKING THE BLOCKS

Making The Flying Geese Units

*Follow **Machine Piecing**, page 57, and **Pressing**, page 58.*

1. Choose 4 matching **rectangles (E)** and 8 assorted **squares (A)**. Draw a diagonal line on wrong side of squares.
2. With right sides together, place 1 square on 1 end of 1 rectangle and stitch along drawn line. Trim $1/4$" from stitching line (**Fig. 1**). Open up and press seam allowances toward triangle (**Fig. 2**).
3. Place another square on opposite end of rectangle. Stitch and trim as before (**Fig. 3**). Open up and press seam allowances toward triangle to make **Flying Geese Unit A**. Make 12 sets of 4 matching Flying Geese Unit A's.

Fig. 1

Fig. 2

Fig. 3

Flying Geese Unit A
(make 12 sets of 4)

4. Repeat Steps 1-3 using 4 medium dark **rectangles** (F) and 8 dark or medium dark **squares** (H) that match rectangles in Flying Geese Unit A to make **Flying Geese Unit B**. Make 12 sets of 4 Flying Geese Unit B's.

Flying Geese Unit B
(make 12 sets of 4)

Making the Triangle-Squares

1. Draw a diagonal line on wrong side of light print **squares (A)**. With right sides together, place 1 light print square on top of 1 dark print **square (C)**. Stitch along drawn line (**Fig. 4**).
2. Trim to a $1/4$" seam allowance along one side of stitching line (**Fig. 5**). Press seam allowances toward darker fabric to make 1 **Triangle-Square**. Make 96 Triangle-Squares.

Making the 4-Patch Units

1. Sew 2 dark **squares (G)** of 1 color and 2 dark or medium dark **squares (G)** of a second color together to make 4-**Patch Unit**. Make 12 4-Patch Units.

Assembling the Blocks

1. Sew 1 **corner square (B)**, 1 **accent square (D)**, and 2 **Triangle-Squares** together to make **Unit 1**. Make 4 Unit 1's. Press the seam allowances toward the squares.
2. Sew **Flying Geese Unit A** and **Flying Geese Unit B** together to make **Unit 2**. Make 4 Unit 2's. Press the seam allowance toward Flying Geese Unit A.
3. Sew 2 **Unit 1's** and 1 **Unit 2** together to make **Row 1**. Make 2 Row 1's. Press seam allowances open.
4. Sew 2 **Unit 2's** and 1 **Four-Patch Unit** together to make **Row 2**. Press seam allowances open.
5. Sew **Row 1's** and **Row 2** together to make **Block**. Press seam allowances open. Block should measure $12^{1}/_{2}$" x $12^{1}/_{2}$" including seam allowances.
6. Repeat Steps 1-5 to make 12 Blocks.

Fig. 4

Fig. 5

Triangle-Square (make 96)

4-Patch Unit (make 12)

Unit 1 (make 4)

Unit 2 (make 4)

Row 1 (make 2)

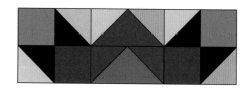

Row 2

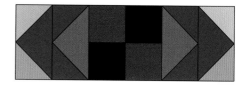

Block (make 12)

ASSEMBLING THE QUILT TOP CENTER

*Refer to **photo**, page 53, for placement.*

1. Sew 4 **sashing squares** and 3 **sashing strips** together to make **Row 1**. Make 5 Row 1's.
2. Sew 4 **sashing strips** and 3 **Blocks** together to make **Row 2**. Make 4 Row 2's.
3. Sew **Rows** together to make quilt top center.

ADDING THE BORDERS

Border #1's

1. Randomly sew 9 beige print **border #1 rectangles** together end to end to make **side border #1** that measures $54^1/_2$" long. Repeat to make another side border #1. Press the seam allowances to one side or open.
2. Folding borders in half to trim equal amounts off each end, refer to **Adding Squared Borders**, page 58, to add **side borders #1** to quilt top center.
3. Randomly sew 8 beige print **border #1 rectangles** together end to end to make **top border #1** that measures $48^1/_2$" long. Repeat to make **bottom border #1**.
4. Repeat Step 2 to sew top and bottom border to quilt top center.

Border #2's

1. Randomly sew **border #2 rectangles** together end to end to make 1 **border #2** strip. Press the seam allowances to 1 side or open.
2. Refer to **Adding Squared Borders**, page 58, to trim and sew **border #2's** to quilt top in same manner as previous.

Border #3's

1. Randomly sew **border #3 rectangles** together end to end to make 1 **border #3** strip. Press the seam allowances to 1 side or open.
2. Trim and sew **border #3's** to quilt top in same manner as border #2's.

COMPLETING THE QUILT

1. Follow **Quilting**, page 59, to mark, layer, and quilt as desired. Quilt shown is machine quilted with an all-over flower and vine pattern.
2. Follow **Making a Hanging Sleeve**, page 61, if a hanging sleeve is desired.
3. Sew **binding strips** together end to end using a diagonal seam (**Fig. 6**) to make a continuous binding strip.
4. Follow **Attaching Binding**, page 62, to bind quilt.

Fig. 6

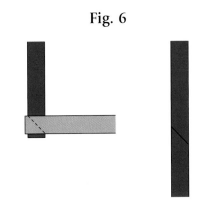

general instructions

To make your quilting easier and more enjoyable, we encourage you to carefully read all of the general instructions, study the color photographs, and familiarize yourself with the individual project instructions before beginning a project.

FABRICS
SELECTING FABRICS

Choose high-quality, medium-weight 100% cotton fabrics. All-cotton fabrics hold a crease better, fray less, and are easier to quilt than cotton/polyester blends.

Yardage requirements listed for each project are based on 43"/44" wide fabric with a "usable" width of 40" after shrinkage and trimming selvages. Actual usable width will probably vary slightly from fabric to fabric. Our recommended yardage lengths should be adequate for occasional re-squaring of fabric when many cuts are required.

PREPARING FABRICS

Pre-washing fabrics may cause edges to ravel. As a result, your precut fabric pieces may not be large enough to cut all of the pieces required for your chosen project. Therefore, we do not recommend pre-washing your yardage or precut fabrics.

Before cutting, prepare fabrics with a steam iron set on cotton and starch or sizing. The starch or sizing will give the fabric a crisp finish. This will make cutting more accurate and may make piecing easier.

ROTARY CUTTING
CUTTING FROM YARDAGE

- Place fabric on work surface with fold closest to you.

- Cut all strips from the selvage-to-selvage width of the fabric.

- Square left edge of fabric using rotary cutter and rulers (**Figs. 1 - 2**).

- To cut each strip required for a project, place ruler over cut edge of fabric, aligning desired marking on ruler with cut edge; make cut (**Fig. 3**).

- When cutting several strips from a single piece of fabric, it is important to make sure that cuts remain at a perfect right angle to the fold; square fabric as needed.

Fig. 1	Fig. 2	Fig. 3
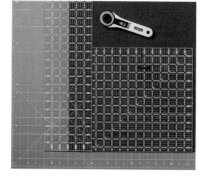		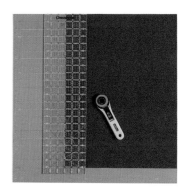

CUTTING FROM FAT QUARTERS

- Place fabric flat on work surface with lengthwise (short) edge closest to you.

- Cut all strips parallel to the long edge of fabric in the same manner as cutting from yardage.

- To cut each strip required for a project, place ruler over cut edge of fabric, aligning desired marking on ruler with cut edge; make cut.

MACHINE PIECING

Precise cutting, followed by accurate piecing, will ensure that all pieces of quilt top fit together well.

- Set sewing machine stitch length for approximately 11 stitches per inch.

- Use neutral-colored general-purpose sewing thread (not quilting thread) in needle and in bobbin.

- An accurate $1/4$" seam allowance is *essential.* Presser feet that are $1/4$" wide are available for most sewing machines.

- When piecing, always place pieces right sides together and match raw edges; pin if necessary.

- Chain piecing saves time and will usually result in more accurate piecing.

- Trim away points of seam allowances that extend beyond edges of sewn pieces.

SEWING STRIP SETS

When there are several strips to assemble into a strip set, first sew strips together into pairs, then sew pairs together to form strip set. To help avoid distortion, sew seams in opposite directions (**Fig. 4**).

SEWING ACROSS SEAM INTERSECTIONS

When sewing across the intersection of two seams, place pieces right sides together and match seams exactly, making sure seam allowances are pressed in opposite directions (**Fig. 5**).

SEWING SHARP POINTS

To ensure sharp points when joining triangular or diagonal pieces, stitch across the center of the "X" (shown in pink) formed on wrong side by previous seams (**Fig. 6**).

Fig. 4

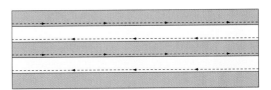

Fig. 5

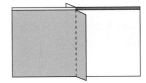

Fig. 6

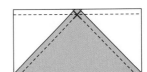

PRESSING

- Use steam iron set on "Cotton" for all pressing.

- Press after sewing each seam.

- Seam allowances are almost always pressed to one side, usually toward darker fabric. However, to reduce bulk it may occasionally be necessary to press seam allowances toward the lighter fabric or even to press them open.

- To prevent dark fabric seam allowance from showing through light fabric, trim darker seam allowance slightly narrower than lighter seam allowance.

- To press long seams, such as those in long strip sets, without curving or other distortion, lay strips across the width of the ironing board.

ADDING SQUARED BORDERS

In most cases, our instructions for cutting borders include an extra 2" of length at each end for "insurance;" borders will be trimmed after measuring completed center section of quilt top.

1. Mark the center of each edge of quilt top.
2. Squared borders are usually added to sides, then top and bottom of the center section of the quilt top. To add side borders, measure the *length* of the quilt top across the center to determine length of borders (**Fig. 7**). Trim side borders to the determined length.
3. Mark center of 1 long edge of side border. Matching center marks and raw edges, pin border to quilt top, easing in any fullness; stitch. Repeat for remaining side border.
4. Measure the *width* of the quilt top across the center, including attached borders, to determine length of top and bottom borders. Trim top and bottom borders to the determined length. Repeat Step 3 to add top and bottom borders to quilt top (**Fig. 8**).

Fig. 7   **Fig. 8**

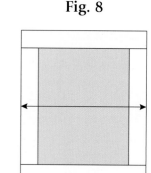

QUILTING

Quilting holds the three layers (top, batting, and backing) of the quilt together and can be done by hand or machine. Because marking, layering, and quilting are interrelated and may be done in different orders depending on circumstances, please read entire Quilting section, pages 59 – 61, before beginning your project.

TYPES OF QUILTING DESIGNS

In the Ditch Quilting
Quilting along seamlines or along edges of appliquéd pieces is called "in the ditch" quilting. This type of quilting should be done on side **opposite** seam allowance and does not have to be marked.

Outline Quilting
Quilting a consistent distance, usually $1/4$", from seam or appliqué is called "outline" quilting. Outline quilting may be marked, or $1/4$" wide masking tape may be placed along seamlines for quilting guide. (Do not leave tape on quilt longer than necessary, since it may leave an adhesive residue.)

Channel Quilting
Quilting with straight, parallel lines is called "channel" quilting. This type of quilting may be marked or stitched using a guide.

Meandering Quilting
Quilting in random curved lines and swirls is called "meandering" quilting. Quilting lines should not cross or touch each other. This type of quilting does not need to be marked.

Stipple Quilting
Meandering quilting that is very closely spaced is called "stipple" quilting. Stippling will flatten the area quilted and is often stitched in background areas to raise appliquéd or pieced designs. This type of quilting does not need to be marked.

MARKING QUILTING LINES
Quilting lines may be marked using fabric marking pencils, chalk markers, or water- or air-soluble pens.

Simple quilting designs may be marked with chalk or chalk pencil after basting. A small area may be marked, then quilted, before moving to next area to be marked. Intricate designs should be marked before basting using a more durable marker.

Caution: Pressing may permanently set some marks. **Test** different markers **on scrap fabric** to find one that marks clearly and can be thoroughly removed.

A wide variety of precut quilting stencils, as well as entire books of quilting patterns, are available. Using a stencil makes it easier to mark intricate or repetitive designs.

To make a stencil from a pattern, center template plastic over pattern and use a permanent marker to trace pattern onto plastic. Use a craft knife with single or double blade to cut channels along traced lines (**Fig. 9**).

Fig. 9

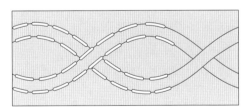

PREPARING THE BACKING

To allow for slight shifting of quilt top during quilting, backing should be approximately 4" larger on all sides. Yardage requirements listed for quilt backings are calculated for 43"/44"w fabric. Using 90"w or 108"w fabric for the backing of a bed-sized quilt may eliminate piecing. To piece a backing using 43"/44"w fabric, use the following instructions.

1. Measure length and width of quilt top; add 8" to each measurement.
2. If determined width is 79" or less, cut backing fabric into two lengths slightly longer than determined *length* measurement. Trim selvages. Place lengths with right sides facing and sew long edges together, forming tube (**Fig. 10**). Match seams and press along one fold (**Fig. 11**). Cut along pressed fold to form single piece (**Fig. 12**).
3. If determined width is more than 79", it may require less fabric yardage if the backing is pieced horizontally. Divide determined *length* measurement by 40" to determine how many widths will be needed. Cut required number of widths the determined *width* measurement. Trim selvages. Sew long edges together to form single piece.
4. Trim backing to size determined in Step 1; press seam allowances open.

Fig. 10	**Fig. 11**	**Fig. 12**
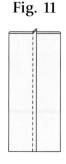		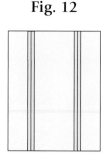

CHOOSING THE BATTING

The appropriate batting will make quilting easier. For fine hand quilting, choose low-loft batting. All cotton or cotton/polyester blend battings work well for machine quilting because the cotton helps "grip" quilt layers. If quilt is to be tied, a high-loft batting, sometimes called extra-loft or fat batting, may be used to make quilt "fluffy."

Types of batting include cotton, polyester, wool, cotton/polyester blend, cotton/wool blend, and silk.

When selecting batting, refer to package labels for characteristics and care instructions. Cut batting same size as prepared backing.

ASSEMBLING THE QUILT

1. Examine wrong side of quilt top closely; trim any seam allowances and clip any threads that may show through front of the quilt. Press quilt top, being careful not to "set" any marked quilting lines.
2. Place backing *wrong* side up on flat surface. Use masking tape to tape edges of backing to surface. Place batting on top of backing fabric. Smooth batting gently, being careful not to stretch or tear. Center quilt top *right* side up on batting.
3. Use 1" rustproof safety pins to "pin-baste" all layers together, spacing pins approximately 4" apart. Begin at center and work toward outer edges to secure all layers. If possible, place pins away from areas that will be quilted, although pins may be removed as needed when quilting.

MACHINE QUILTING METHODS

Use general-purpose thread in the bobbin. Do not use quilting thread. Thread the needle with general-purpose thread or transparent monofilament thread to make quilting blend with quilt top fabrics. Use decorative thread, such as a metallic or contrasting-color general-purpose thread, to make quilting lines stand out more.

Straight-Line Quilting

The term "straight-line" is somewhat deceptive, since curves (especially gentle ones) as well as straight lines can be stitched with this technique.

1. Set the stitch length for six to ten stitches per inch and attach a walking foot to the sewing machine.
2. Determine which section of the quilt will have the longest continuous quilting line, oftentimes area from center top to center bottom. Roll up and secure each edge of the quilt to help reduce the bulk, keeping fabrics smooth. Smaller projects may not need to be rolled.
3. Begin stitching on longest quilting line, using very short stitches for the first $1/4$" to "lock" quilting. Stitch across project, using one hand on each side of walking foot to slightly spread fabric and to guide fabric through machine. Lock stitches at end of quilting line.
4. Continue machine quilting, stitching longer quilting lines first to stabilize quilt before moving on to other areas.

Free-Motion Quilting

Free-motion quilting may be free form or may follow a marked pattern.

1. Attach a darning foot to the sewing machine and lower or cover feed dogs.
2. Position the quilt under the darning foot; lower foot. Holding top thread, take a stitch and pull bobbin thread to top of quilt. To "lock" beginning of quilting line, hold top and bobbin threads while making three to five stitches in place.
3. Use one hand on each side of darning foot to slightly spread fabric and to move fabric through the machine. Even stitch length is achieved by using smooth, flowing hand motion and steady machine speed. Slow machine speed and fast hand movement will create long stitches. Fast machine speed and slow hand movement will create short stitches. Move quilt sideways, back and forth, in a circular motion, or in a random motion to create desired designs; do not rotate quilt. Lock stitches at end of each quilting line.

MAKING A HANGING SLEEVE

Attaching a hanging sleeve to the back of a quilt before the binding is added allows project to be displayed on a wall.

1. Measure the width of the quilt top edge and subtract 1". Cut a piece of fabric 7"w by the determined measurement.
2. Press short edges of fabric piece $1/4$" to wrong side; press edges $1/4$" to the wrong side again and machine stitch in place.
3. Matching wrong sides, fold piece in half lengthwise to form a tube.
4. Follow project instructions to sew binding to quilt top and to trim backing and batting. Before Blindstitching binding to backing, match raw edges and stitch hanging sleeve to center top edge on back of quilt.
5. Finish binding quilt, treating hanging sleeve as part of binding.
6. Blindstitch bottom of hanging sleeve to backing, taking care not to stitch through to front of quilt.

ATTACHING BINDING

1. Matching wrong sides, press binding in half lengthwise.
2. Beginning with one end near center on bottom edge of quilt, lay binding around quilt to make sure that seams in binding will not end up at a corner. Adjust placement if necessary. Matching raw edges of binding to raw edge of quilt top, pin binding to right side of quilt along one edge.
3. When you reach first corner, mark $1/4$" from corner of quilt top (**Fig. 13**).
4. Beginning approximately 10" from end of binding and using $1/4$" seam allowance, sew binding to quilt, backstitching at beginning of stitching and at mark (**Fig. 14**). Lift needle out of fabric and clip thread.
5. Fold binding as shown in **Figs. 15 – 16** and pin binding to adjacent side, matching raw edges. When you've reached the next corner, mark $1/4$" from edge of quilt top.
6. Backstitching at edge of quilt top, sew pinned binding to quilt (**Fig. 17**); backstitch at the next mark. Lift needle out of fabric and clip thread.
7. Continue sewing binding to quilt, stopping approximately 10" from starting point (**Fig. 18**).
8. Bring beginning and end of binding to center of opening and fold each end back, leaving a $1/4$" space between folds (**Fig. 19**). Finger press folds.

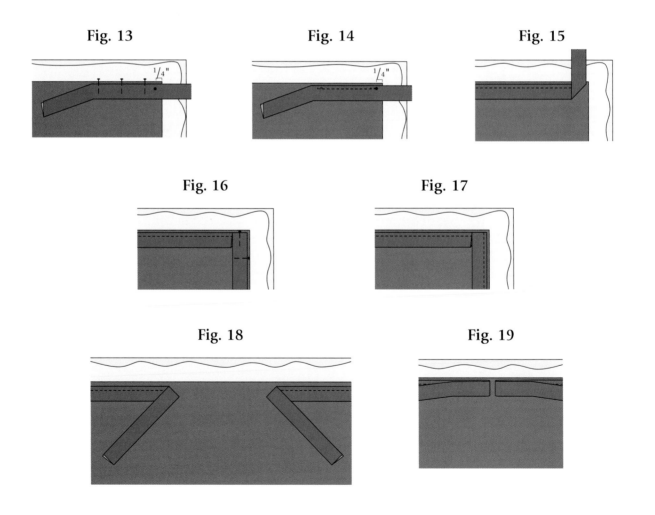

Fig. 13   Fig. 14   Fig. 15

Fig. 16   Fig. 17

Fig. 18   Fig. 19

9. Unfold ends of binding and draw a line across wrong side in finger-pressed crease. Draw a line through the lengthwise pressed fold of binding at the same spot to create a cross mark. With edge of ruler at cross mark, line up 45° angle marking on ruler with one long side of binding. Draw a diagonal line from edge to edge. Repeat on remaining end, making sure that the two diagonal lines are angled the same way (**Fig. 20**).

10. Matching right sides and diagonal lines, pin binding ends together at right angles (**Fig. 21**).

11. Machine stitch along diagonal line (**Fig. 22**), removing pins as you stitch.

12. Lay binding against quilt to double check that it is correct length. **13.** Trim binding ends, leaving ¹/₄" seam allowance; press seam open. Stitch binding to quilt.

14. Trim backing and batting a scant ¹/₄" larger than quilt top so that batting and backing will fill the binding when it is folded over to quilt backing.

15. On one edge of quilt, fold binding over to quilt backing and pin pressed edge in place, covering stitching line (**Fig. 23**). On adjacent side, fold binding over, forming a mitered corner (**Fig. 24**). Repeat to pin remainder of binding in place.

16. Blindstitch binding to backing, taking care not to stitch through to front of quilt.

Fig. 20   **Fig. 21**

Fig. 22   **Fig. 23**   **Fig. 24**

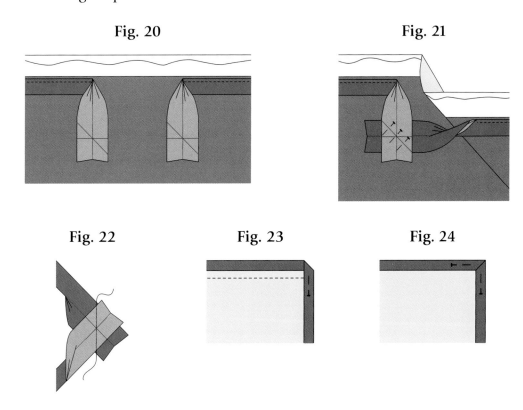

SIGNING AND DATING YOUR QUILT

A completed quilt is a work of art and should be signed and dated. There are many different ways to do this and numerous books on the subject. The label should reflect the style of the quilt, the occasion or person for which it was made, and the quilter's own particular talents. The following are suggestions for recording the history of a quilt or adding a sentiment for future generations.

- Embroider quilter's name, date, and any additional information on quilt top or backing. Matching floss, such as cream floss on white border, will leave a subtle record. Bright or contrasting floss will make the information stand out.

- Make a label from muslin and use a permanent marker to write information. Use different colored permanent markers to make the label more decorative. Stitch the label to back of the quilt.

- Use photo-transfer paper to add an image to white or cream fabric label. Stitch the label to the back of the quilt.

- Piece an extra block from quilt top pattern to use as a label. Add information with a permanent fabric pen. Appliqué the block to the back of the quilt.

BLIND STITCH

Come up at 1, go down at 2, and come up at 3 (**Fig. 25**). Length of stitches may be varied as desired.

Fig. 25

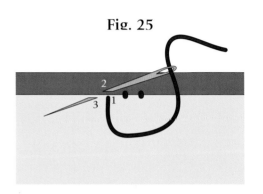

Metric Conversion Chart	
Inches x 2.54 = centimeters (cm)	Yards x .9144 = meters (m)
Inches x 25.4 = millimeters (mm)	Yards x 91.44 = centimeters (cm)
Inches x .0254 = meters (m)	Centimeters x .3937 = inches (")
	Meters x 1.0936 = yards (yd)

Standard Equivalents					
1/8"	3.2 mm	0.32 cm	1/8 yard	11.43 cm	0.11 m
1/4"	6.35 mm	0.635 cm	1/4 yard	22.86 cm	0.23 m
3/8"	9.5 mm	0.95 cm	3/8 yard	34.29 cm	0.34 m
1/2"	12.7 mm	1.27 cm	1/2 yard	45.72 cm	0.46 m
5/8"	15.9 mm	1.59 cm	5/8 yard	57.15 cm	0.57 m
3/4"	19.1 mm	1.91 cm	3/4 yard	68.58 cm	0.69 m
7/8"	22.2 mm	2.22 cm	7/8 yard	80 cm	0.8 m
1"	25.4 mm	2.54 cm	1 yard	91.44 cm	0.91 m